MOTOCROSS CYCLES

BY LINDSAY SHAFFER

EPIC

BELLWETHER MEDIA

EPIC BOOKS are no ordinary books. They burst with intense action, high-speed heroics, and shadows of the unknown. Are you ready for an Epic adventure?

This edition first published in 2019 by Bellwether Media, Inc.

No part of this publication may be reproduced in whole or in part without written permission of the publisher. For information regarding permission, write to Bellwether Media, Inc., Attention: Permissions Department, 6012 Blue Circle Drive, Minnetonka, MN 55343.

Library of Congress Cataloging-in-Publication Data

Names: Shaffer, Lindsay, author.
Title: Motocross Cycles / by Lindsay Shaffer.
Description: Minneapolis, MN : Bellwether Media, Inc., 2019. | Includes
   bibliographical references and index. | Audience: Ages 7-12. | Audience: Grades 2 to 7
Identifiers: LCCN 2018002174 (print) | LCCN 2018007137 (ebook) | ISBN
   9781626178755 (hardcover : alk. paper)| ISBN 9781681036229 (ebook)
Subjects: LCSH: Trail bikes–Juvenile literature. | Motocross–Juvenile literature.
Classification: LCC TL441 (ebook) | LCC TL441 .S53 2019 (print) | DDC 629.227/5–dc23
LC record available at https://lccn.loc.gov/2018002174

Editor: Christina Leaf   Designer: Jeffrey Kollock

Printed in the United States of America, North Mankato, MN

TABLE OF CONTENTS

HIGH-SPEED EXCITEMENT!

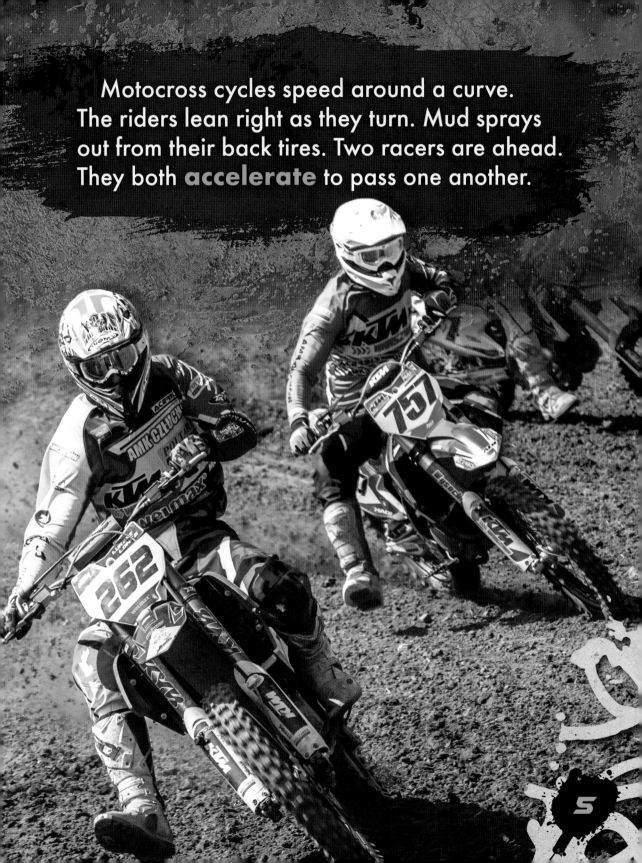

Motocross cycles speed around a curve. The riders lean right as they turn. Mud sprays out from their back tires. Two racers are ahead. They both **accelerate** to pass one another.

The racers bounce over **whoops**. Then, they fly over a **table top** jump.

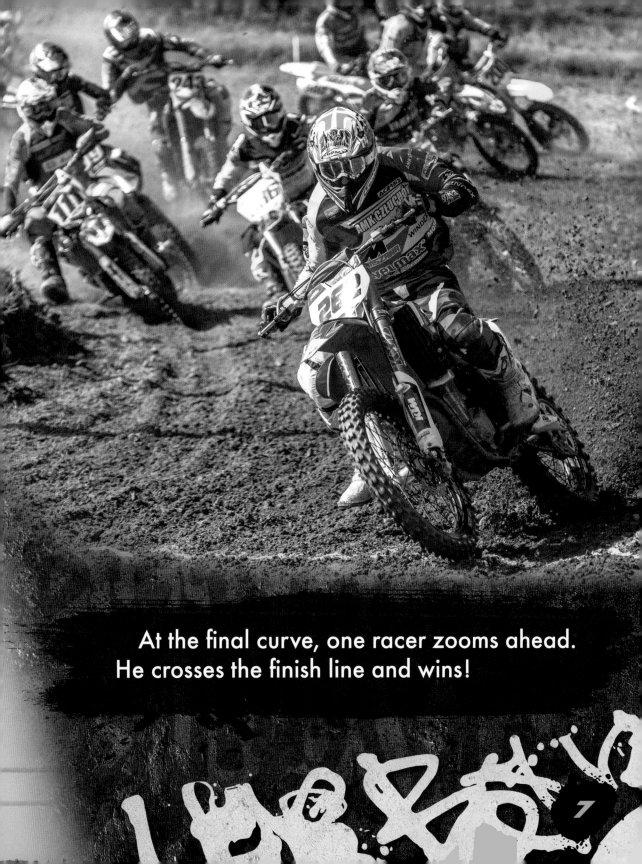

At the final curve, one racer zooms ahead.
He crosses the finish line and wins!

WHAT ARE MOTOCROSS CYCLES?

Motocross cycles are a type of dirt bike. They have lightweight parts to make them faster. People ride them in motocross and **supercross** races. They race on dirt tracks with curves and jumps.

supercross

HILLS AND VALLEYS

Motocross tracks have different sections. These include hills, curves, whoops, and jumps.

Motocross cycles are also used for **freestyle** contests. Their light weight makes them great for jumping.

10

Freestyle riders do tricks and flips in midair. They even create their own tricks!

THE HISTORY OF MOTOCROSS CYCLES

In the 1920s, motorcycle racing became popular in Great Britain. Soon, the sport spread throughout Europe. Companies began making special bikes for motocross races. These motocross cycles could race faster and jump higher.

motocross in England, 1925

MOTOCROSS TIMELINE

The Netherlands holds the first Motocross des Nations race

1947

1924

First official motocross-style race takes place in Great Britain

1972

American Motorcycle Association creates the AMA Motocross Championship

1999

Freestyle motocross becomes part of the X Games

Motocross came to the United States in the 1960s. In the 1970s, motocross and supercross became popular sports. The X Games brought freestyle riding to the spotlight. Today, riders can compete in many different events.

MOTOCROSS CYCLE PARTS

Motocross cycles have bumpy tires. The bumps add **traction**. Strong **suspension systems** allow for safe landings after big jumps. Safety gear also protects riders. Everyone wears a helmet, goggles, and boots.

flip lever

GET A GRIP!

Freestyle motocross cycles often have flip levers on their handlebars. Riders use them to do tricks.

17

18

Motocross cycle engines are powerful. They come in sizes like 125 **cubic centimeters** (cc) and 250cc. Larger numbers usually mean more power. Motocross cycles have fewer parts and lighter frames than other dirt bikes. This gives them extra speed.

IDENTIFY A MOTOCROSS CYCLE

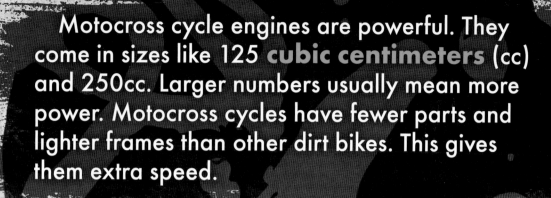

light body

suspension system

powerful engine

bumpy tires

MOTOCROSS CYCLE COMPETITIONS

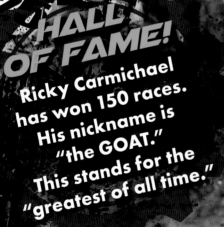

HALL OF FAME!

Ricky Carmichael has won 150 races. His nickname is "the GOAT." This stands for the "greatest of all time."

Motocross contests range from small town races to X Games events. Step Up challenges riders to soar over higher and higher jumps. Riders show off their skills in Best Trick. They invent new tricks every year!

Step Up

GLOSSARY

accelerate—to go faster

cubic centimeters—units used to measure volume

freestyle—related to events in which riders do tricks and stunts to earn points

supercross—motocross races held indoors

suspension systems—systems of springs, tires, and shocks that cushion a vehicle's ride

table top—a type of jump with a flat middle section

traction—the ability to grip a surface while moving

whoops—a series of small hills on a motocross track

22

TO LEARN MORE

AT THE LIBRARY

Adamson, Thomas K. *Motocross Freestyle*. Minneapolis, Minn.: Bellwether Media, 2016.

Adamson, Thomas K. *Motocross Racing*. Minneapolis, Minn.: Bellwether Media, 2016.

Hamilton, John. *Motocross*. Minneapolis, Minn.: A&D Xtreme, 2015.

ON THE WEB

Learning more about motocross cycles is as easy as 1, 2, 3.

1. Go to www.factsurfer.com.

2. Enter "motocross cycles" into the search box.

3. Click the "Surf" button and you will see a list of related web sites.

With factsurfer.com, finding more information is just a click away.

The images in this book are reproduced through the courtesy of: tarczas, front cover, pp. 1, 4-5, 6, 7, 16-17; EvrenKalinbacak, p. 8; Maciej Kopaniecki, pp. 8-9; Pukhov K, p. 10; ermess, p. 11; Heritage Images/ Getty Images, pp. 12, 14 (Motocross Des Nations); Hulton Deutsch/ Getty Images, pp. 12-13; Anatoliy Evankov, pp. 14-15; RacingOne/ Getty Images, p. 15 (AMA); David Madison/ Getty Images, p. 15 (X Games); Christian Bertran, p. 16; takoburito, pp. 18-19; KTM Press Center, p. 19 (bike); smileimage9, pp. 20-21; Zuma Press, Inc./ Alamy, p. 21.